Horse Training Basics 101

Beginner's Guide to Horsemanship, Training and Safety

Sue Jordan

This book is dedicated to Dad who taught me everything I know and love about horses.

Speedy Publishing LLC (c) 2014
40 E. Main St., #1156
Newark, DE 19711
www.speedypublishing.co

Ordering Information:
Quantity sales; Special discounts are available on quantity purchases by corporations, associations, and others. For details, contact the "Special Sales Department" at the address above.

This is a reprint book.

Manufactured in the United States of America

TABLE OF CONTENTS

PUBLISHER'S NOTES

i

CHAPTER 1: INTRODUCTION TO HORSE OWNERSHIP

If you are reading this book, you are either looking to buy a horse or maybe you have already acquired a horse. Either way the horse will need to be trained. Whether you do it yourself or hire a trainer to train the horse for you.

You already know the cost of purchasing a horse can range from about $1000 to $20,000. You may have estimated the cost of feeding, shoeing, and health care to run you about $2,000 per year. That $2,000 per year is if you have property in the country and will keep the horse with you. If you are planning on boarding your horse, then you can expect an additional $2,000 to $3,000 per year.

Assuming you are planning on riding your horse an average of 350 hours per year, you will want to include in all those expenses; the cost of your health insurance and possible time off from work. Since you are asking yourself, "Why?" you need to factor in health insurance and time off from work, I will explain. There are thousands of people each year that receive injuries from horseback riding. Twenty-five percent of those injuries happen to children who are 16 years of age and younger. Many of the head injuries lead to brain injury.

The brain injuries can cause serious damages that have a lifelong effect. Unfortunately we are not talking about injuries caused riding in rodeos. The majority of these mishaps occur during recreational riding. Eighty percent of the fatal accidents occur at normal horse speeds and are not caused because the horse bucked or reared up.

As it turns out you are safer riding a motorcycle than you are on the back of a horse. Researchers tell us that motorcyclists average 7,000 hours of riding time per serious accident, while horseback riders can expect an accident to happen for every 350 hours of riding time.

The best method of stopping injury accidents is education. A properly trained horse is less likely to misbehave, and he will be a much safer animal to ride if he has been taught not to behave in a way that will cause a serious injuries. These actions will include biting, kicking, or running away with a rider. A well-trained horse will be much more patient with the odd habits of the untrained person.

Riding on the back of an untrained horse is like driving a car that does not have any brakes. You can take them out for a test run, but you may come back dead. Even though the horse's intentions are good, if he doesn't have experience, you are riding around with a creature that weighs over a thousand pounds and likes to do whatever he wants. As an investment, horses are more of a liability. The horse has the potential of hurting someone and his resale value is next to nothing.

If you have an untrained horse, he can be dangerous. You probably didn't buy him just to put him out to pasture and get fat and lazy.

Just remember training your horse makes your horse more accessible to you as well as being useful and safer to be around.

If you don't have the time or experience to train a horse, you can hire a trainer. Depending on the training the horse needs, training can take anywhere from two months to a year to be trained. The end result is that you will have a horse that is well trained. However you will still be untrained unless you are already an experienced rider. If you are not an experienced rider this means you will have to find training for yourself.

For a whole lot less money than you will pay for a trainer, you can train a horse on your own. You will both be learning at the same time. Of course the horse will not be ready to ride for a portion of that time, but you will learn some things before you get on the back of that horse.

Here are some tips for the novice horseback rider.

- If this is the first time you have owned a horse, it would be a good idea to pay a professional trainer to help you choose the right horse before you shell out the money for a horse.
- You will always want to supervise children when they are around horses. Make sure the children are not in the line of fire should the horse decide to kick.
- If you have children, you will want them to know all about horse safety.
- When you are looking for a saddle to purchase, make sure to purchase a saddle that has release catches to ensure a fallen rider will not be dragged by the horse because of a foot caught in the stirrups.
- Make sure you invest in an equestrian helmet that meets the ASTM standards.

- Do not allow a horse to nibble or "kiss" you, not even a young horse. This can turn into biting and is very hard to stop.
- Do not wear any loose fitting clothes. It may catch on tack, branches or fences.

Never sneak up on a horse from behind.

CHAPTER 2: ADVICE ON PURCHASING YOUR FIRST HORSE

If you haven't already made the purchase of a horse, here is something you might want to keep in mind. Have a vet go with you to look at the horse before finalizing the purchase. As the vet is looking over the horse, let him tell you what he learns about the horse. You will have the opportunity to ask the vet questions about the horse. If the vet does not feel the horse is right for you, listen to him when he tells you not to buy the horse.

If the horse you are looking at has a certain temperament, specific training or lack of training, the vet may recommend that you not purchase that particular horse. Being a new horse owner the vet will recognize that you could have trouble with the horse later on down the road. Take for example; a well-trained cutting horse is not necessarily a suitable pleasure riding horse because they were trained to do a specific job.

By taking a vet with you to look at a horse, you will not only be paying for a check-up for the horse, but also for the vet's expertise with horses. Some people may believe that it isn't a vet's business to find the proper match for you, however you and the horse you purchase or don't purchase will be better off. So, if you take a vet with you to look at a horse, it is best to listen to him. He may tell you, if you purchase a particular horse, that the horse will need a professional trainer.

Many sellers like to attend when the vet check's the horse, but they prefer the seller say nothing during the examination. The seller could influence your perceptions and do nothing for your confidence.

The vet will also check the horse for any physical ailments. This will prevent you from buying a horse with an existing condition that may prevent the horse from performing, as you would like for him to do. If you buy a horse to ride, you don't want to end up with a horse whose legs can no longer sustain the weight of a rider, or spends the majority of your time and money with the vet.

If the horse has an existing condition you are aware of, ask the vet to check it out. The vet may decline or he will inform you of the problems associated with the condition before moving on to something else. Vets use professional ethics and many times will not report on a horse belonging to an existing client because of conflict of interests.

When it comes down to the vet check, many people don't want to listen to someone else's advice and will not have the vet perform a check-up before making the purchase. New horse owners on the other hand should know that having a vet check the horse can save you thousand if not tens of thousands of dollar by not purchasing the wrong horse.

CHAPTER 3: ASSUMPTIONS TO AVOID AS A NEW HORSE OWNER

Mistake #1 – Assuming you can ride any horse.

Horses are not all the same. Some will let you get on and you can ride them easily. While others are so green that you could get hurt if you have little or no riding experience. The horses that will let just about anyone on and ride are usually the older horses. Because they have been ridden the most they will be the most forgiving of the mistakes that a beginning rider can make. The younger horses are a lot tougher to ride unless they have been completely broke.

Mistake #2 – Assuming there is only one-way to train a horse.

When an experienced horse owner starts having problems with their horse, they will look for answers and ask questions. One of the first places they look is in books. When the author of the book explains a training technique, the new horse owner assumes it is the same technique used by all horse trainers. After trying the technique and the new horse owner can't train their horse, then they tend to think they have a dumb horse or a horse that can't be trained. Usually there is more than one way to train a horse. So if you are using one technique that doesn't seem to be working, then you will need to try something else. Usually by finding a book or video created by a different trainer the methods they use will be different than the methods you are trying.

Mistake #3 – Not riding the horse enough.

As a new horse owner if you are having trouble with your horse, chances are the horse has not gone sour, but because the horse needs you to ride him more often. A horse needs to be ridden a lot to make them a good riding horse. So the best thing you can do for your horse is to ride him, ride him and ride him. Every couple of weeks is not enough riding for a horse.

Mistake #4 – Thinking the horse is at fault when there is a problem.

Horses are not unlike any other creature they have their problems. Usually many of the problems you will see with a horse are the owner's fault. You will have to look at the problem you are having with the horse to assess the reason behind the problem. In many cases it could be you don't have the control over him you need to have. There are various different methods you can use to create control.

Mistake #5 – The horse owner lacks the understanding how the horse thinks.

Because horses are not cats or dogs, they don't think like them. Horses are a prey animal meaning they run from anything that scares them. Their "flight instinct" has been ingrained into them for thousands of years. If you are training your horse, you will need lots of patience and understanding that they are just naturally afraid of almost everything.

Mistake #6 – The new horse owner doesn't know that every interaction with their horse is a training exercise.

Whether you are petting him, brushing him or just grooming him you are training him. As a new and inexperienced horse owner you must stop and think about what you do and how you do it because the horse is a lot like your child, he will pick up things from you. You have more of an effect on your horse's behavior than you may be aware of.

Mistake #7 – As a new horse owner if you ride your horse when you have little or no experience of horsemanship, will do more harm than good.

Many new horse owners will ride their horse with no horse-riding training or skills. Horses react to leg pressure, how you sit in the saddle, whether or not the rider is tense and several other signals, so it is important that you have an understanding of riding procedures.

If you want to be successful with your horse, you need to have an understanding about him. If you don't know how to ride, it is best if you take riding lessons and learn how to ride before you ride your horse. You also need to learn how horses think, the best way to shape a horse's behavior, and consistently ride your horse.

CHAPTER 4: TIPS FOR THE NEW TRAINER

Training of a horse is a gradual process of getting your horse's attention and teaching him what you want him to do. You want the horse to think of you as its lead mare no matter the gender of the horse or the owner. Your horse may be a natural leader, which can make training a challenge.

Naturally a horse wants a leader to show them how things are and what to do. It is all part of being a herd animal. So it goes without saying, that you are the one to be the leader in this scenario. A horse will think of you as a leader out of fear or respect. However you want to lead by earning the respect of your horse through your interactions and relationship.

A horse will typically not receive any formal training until they are two years old. Foals however can learn how to behave around people at an early age. Spending as much time as you can with your horse will get him used to being around you, and then by association with people.

Once your horse is old enough to start training, you will start off with groundwork. You are not to attempt to ride him. The horse is not ready to ride. Lunging, or ground training with a long lead rope is the first step in the training process. The lunge line attaches to the horse's halter and allows the horse to move in a large circle while you teach him commands.

Another important lesson for your horse is to teach him how to walk beside you on a lead. Lead training includes teaching the horse to turn and stop at your command. This is crucial and you will use it daily with your horse. Some horses will test you during lead training by trying to shoulder you out of his space. Don't ever let him get away with that. If he resists this simple training, additional training in the future will be difficult.

Horses must be trained so they will accept being ridden, and they must learn to follow the signals of the rider. Your horse needs to respond when it is asked to do something. This will prevent the need for whips or crops to punish or encourage the horse to do as you ask. There is no set time for training sessions, so you don't have to worry about the training sessions being too long or too short. However remember the horse will need breaks.

The beginning of the training session should be used to warm up the horse both physically and mentally. The horse will need time to loosen up joints and warm up its muscles. Usually lunging is used as a method of warming up the horse.

The second part of the training session should cover everything the horse has learned from previous lessons. New skills can be added as a tiny alteration of something the horse already knows. Building on previously learned skills is the key to successfully training your horse.

When adding new equipment such as a saddle, you want the horse to see it, but then after a few minutes you need to take it away. You will need to repeat this for several days. You want the horse to get used to the new piece of equipment so he will not be afraid of it. You will remove the stirrups and leathers at first. Let the horse see the saddle and then hold the saddle over him. Do not touch him with the saddle until he has lost his fear of it. The first time you place the saddle on your horse be prepared for a lot of reassuring and stroking.

The next time you place the saddle on the horse, you will need to add the girth, then the leathers and the stirrups. Only add each new piece of the saddle after the horse has lost his fear of the last piece of the saddle you introduced. This will take some time so don't become impatient.

Finally let the horse wear it during warm-up lunging. Once he is familiar to wearing a saddle, have someone sit on him for a moment as he stands still. Work up to lunging with a rider on his back. Add new things, but only for short periods of time.

Another piece of equipment you will need to add gradually is the bit. The horse needs to become familiar with a bit in its mouth, and just like the saddle this is a long process. The horse will have to become accustom to swallowing saliva with a foreign object in its mouth. To smooth the progress a trainer will slowly introduce a mouthing bit, for just a few minutes at first and slowly build up until the horse will accept it and will stop rejecting it.

All training sessions should end with a cool down period. You will want the cool down period to start when the training session is going well and before the horse becomes tired and frustrated. The cool down period will allow the horse time to mentally and physically wind down and to relax. You want the training sessions to be remembered by the horse as a pleasant experience. By ending the training session on a positive note, helps the horse remember pleasant things about the training session. Now is a good time to allow the horse time to play then return him to the pasture or stable.

You will need to keep in mind the horse takes its cue from you, so it is important that you stay calm and unafraid. Your horse will feel calm and unafraid also. If you move, the horse will sense the change of direction from you, the lead mare, and will follow. Once the horse has learned your body language, he will naturally follow your lead.

In horse training there are rules to direct you on how to work with and train your horse. Horse training is a science and an art.

When you are training your horse to do what you have asked, once he has done it you don't want to repeat the same command and make him repeat the action too many times. The horse will become sour with that command and action, which will make him unwilling to do it again. Once he has done what you have asked, ask him to do it a few more times and move onto something else. You can repeat the command and make him repeat the action another day, but not too many times in one day. You want the training session to be interesting for him. You don't want your horse to become bored with training.

Another thing you will want to do is assess your horse's disposition before you start working with him. You want to know what the student is like before you begin educating him.

If the horse seems nervous, then you need to be quick to reward him. You want to keep his confidence high so make sure you caress him often. You will need to be careful when using aids.

If your horse has a willful disposition, then you will need to be persistent and patient in trying to get him to do what you have asked.

As a trainer it is important to know what your horse's temperament is. It is up to you to help your horse learn the things you are asking him to do.

CHAPTER 5: THE MOST IMPORTANT THING TO UNDERSTAND ABOUT YOUR HORSE

Horses do not have the ability to reason, which is the reason horse training is such a challenge. You have to understand how they think so you will know what works and the reason it works.

The secret to making a horse trainable is their fear of pain and punishment, which has been over the centuries instilled in their minds. We can use that fear to our advantage to teach a horse what we want him to do.

We know about horse's fear; however we can't abuse that knowledge by pushing the horse too far with his fear. It can and usually will backfire on you. Once it backfires you will have trouble with the horse you are trying to train.

One of the first lessons a horse needs to learn is to have confidence in you. Without the confidence in you, the horse will never trust you. Both of these things are the keys to horse training.

There are several ways to teach the horse to have confidence in you. Here is one that's been around since the 1800s. It is also the easiest way to teach your horse to have confidence in you.

This confidence lesson takes advantage of but never abuses the horse's fear. The fear is harnessed in a way and is carefully used to get the horse's confidence in you. It is not much different from getting a child to watch a scary movie and being there to protect him when he gets scared.

When the horse gets scared you need to be there to protect him and tell him everything is okay. You can sooth his fears by petting him and talking to him with a pleasant tone of voice. Essentially you will become the horse's superhero and he will come to depend on that.

Here is an example that will give you an idea of what I'm talking about. A person is riding with a group of people and they come across a large creek. Everyone else's horse crosses the water with no problems, but one person's horse won't cross the creek.

The rider gets upset and starts booting his horse in the ribs. The poor horse wants to do as the rider is asking, but the running water has him scared. The horse starts pacing back and forth, occasionally sniffing at the water but won't cross it. The whole time the rider is still kicking the horse in the ribs.

If the rider had stopped to think about it, he may have realized that the horse was just scared and not being disobedient. The horse needed his help. The horse needed him to talk to him in a soothing voice and pet him.

16

By doing what he did, the rider just gave the horse another reason to fear the running water. Not only is he going to continue to be afraid of running water, but is also afraid he is going to be punished for it.

Now let's look at it from the horse's point of view.

You are a horse that cannot reason. You're instincts are self-preservation. Fear keeps the self-preservation in check. Fear makes you run from danger. It is that fear that keeps you alive.

As the horse, you are standing at the edge of the running water. You dare not cross it because you think there is danger. On top of that you have a person on your back who is pissed off and kicking you in the ribs because you won't step into the water and continue moving forward.

Now you are not only afraid of the running water, but you are feeling punished too. You want to obey, but your instincts are too strong and tell you not to.

If the rider of that horse had realized his horse was afraid as they approached the water and realized it wasn't disobedience causing him not to cross the water, the rider could have spoken softly in a soothing tone of voice. He could have pet the horse and let him know it was okay. He could even have let the horse sniff the water and check it out for himself.

Instead, the rider now has a confused, scared horse who is feeling punished and is less trusting of the rider. The end of this story could have been different, if the rider had reacted different. Remember your horse is counting on you to be their superhero and that means knowing the difference between them being scared and them being disobedient.

CHAPTER 6: TEACHING YOUR HORSE VOICE COMMANDS

For those of you who are inexperienced with horses, voice commands are words, but to the horse they are only sounds. Because horses cannot speak our language, you will need to stop and think about what you will say to your horse when you want a certain reaction from him.

As an example, we are going to look at the word "whoa". This is probably the most abused word in horse language. The "whoa" command to the horse should tell the horse to stop. Unfortunately there are many riders who use the word "whoa" to make the horse slow down, and not stop. The horse will then become conditioned to slow down instead of stop when he hears "whoa". The rider then thinks he has a stupid horse because the horse won't stop when he says "whoa". When actually it is the rider/trainers fault.

If you tell the horse a command that means one thing and you want the horse to do another, basically you are lying to your horse. Lying to your horse will not get you what you want from him. So the best policy is to never lie to your horse. This means when you say "whoa" you intend the horse to stop and not to slow down.

When using voice commands you want to use simple words with as few syllables as possible. So if you want to your horse to back up then you would say "back". If you want your horse to walk, then you will say, "walk". You get the idea.

When you are using a voice command associate an action with the voice command. If you want to teach your horse to gallop, then when are in the round pen you will use one of your aids to teach him to gallop. You say the word "gallop" then you will bring in your aid to motivate your horse to a higher speed.

To teach your horse to walk, you will turn the opposite direction in the round pen and walk. If he goes to fast tell him to "walk" to have him go slower. Also by making a very slight move to the front of him to show him to go slower. After he has walked around the pen a few times, then you will want to stop and pet him.

You must also be careful when you talk to your horse. Don't use the voice commands in a threatening tone of voice or by yelling a command. You will scare and confuse your horse and increase his heart rate. He may take longer to train.

"Step" is a popular command to teach a horse. You use this command to make the horse move forward, to take a step. Don't yell the command at your horse because your horse may take it as a punishment, and it may take longer for the horse to understand what it is you want him to do.

CHAPTER 7: HOW TO LEAD AND EARN YOUR HORSE'S RESPECT

The animal kingdom has a pecking order, which is very similar to our military. In the military the ranks in pecking order is General down to Private. The General will make the decisions on where to go and what to do, etc.

The rank beneath the General will act like the General, but he will not give orders to the General because it is the General that orders him. This continues on down the ranks to the bottom of the list. When a new animal joins a group the pecking order shifts. You can use this information to your advantage. You want to make yourself the leader in your horse's eyes. You want him to look to you for direction and he will obey you.

It will be instinct for a dominant horse to let a more dominant being make the decisions. The dominant being in this case would be you. You will become the leader by using body language to show you are confident. Dominant and aggressive are not the same thing. You want to be dominant not aggressive.

If you have a horse that is a General, you may have to become more assertive. You don't want the horse to perceive you as a threat. It can be easy to come across as threatening when you are trying to be assertive, but if the horse feels threatened, he will fight back. You won't be able to win, when the horse fights back.

When they are in the wild, dominant and aggressive horses will tighten their bodies and move quickly with fury to get into another horse's space. The weaker of the two horses will give in and move out of the space. This is similar to the General screaming an order at the Private and the Private obeys.

When horses are relaxed they express this with slow movement, relaxed and slow steps. Slow movement will draw one horse to another. This is also how they welcome other horses into their space.

When your horse is trying to show you he's the General, he will show this by a clamped-down tail with pinned ears. To get him to accept you as the General you will move him out of his space. To do this you must match any quick moves his makes with quick moves of your own. You want to make the first strike before he does.

You can do this with a quick arm movement towards him – almost like you are violently shooing away some pesky flies. If your horse is being aggressive, you can use an aggressive tone of voice towards the horse.

You will be able to tell he has given in to you when he turns his head or drops it, relaxes his tail and begins to chew or takes a deep breath. When your horse does this he is basically saying, "Okay, I'll do what you say because I want to listen to you." You must pay attention for these signals because they will let you know your horse is in the Private mode and not in the General mode.

After going into the round pen to train your horse, check how he responds to you. If he rubs his head on you or swings his rear end towards you then he is challenging your position as General. If you have a horse that is not dominant, make sure he has confidence. Be extra careful not to be threatening to him in any way.

CHAPTER 8: UNDERSTANDING THE METHOD BEHIND LEAD TRAINING

The lead rope that attaches to the halter of the horse does not control the horse, and they won't lead horses. The lead rope lets you communicate the speed, the direction and the shape you want the horse to move.

The easiest exercise is teaching the horse to stop. You can accomplish this anywhere by walking the horse around and every now and then stand still, giving your horse the command to "stand". Do not pull backwards on the lead rope when you stop. You only need to use a little resistance pressure.

Your horse may at first stop in front, but the hindquarters may move a quarter circle. As you continue to work with him he will learn to come to a complete stop.

These early lessons should only last about 10 to 15 minutes. You can start teaching this while he is still a foal.

You can start this lesson by taking your horse to a small indoor arena. Bringing the horse to an indoor arena will mean fewer distractions than an outdoor arena. This will make it easier to keep your horse's attention.

The first time in an arena your horse will want to check everything out. Go ahead and let your horse play and run. Don't try to direct where he goes. It is best you just follow him around.

You can use his playtime as a play lesson, which you will want to repeat. By using consistent movements you will establish two concepts that will become logical to your horse. As you are walking around shoulder to shoulder with horse facing the same direction he is, you teach him a direction of forward motion. When you turn towards the horse, this will help teach the horse to stop and stand.

After the horse understands these two concepts, you will be able to turn from facing his shoulder to facing with him in the same direction and encourage him to walk with you. You can do this by making obvious moves with your feet. You will build on these concepts gradually to lead the horse forward or ask him to stop and stand whenever and wherever you need him to.

Teaching a horse to back-up is important, and don't think that taking one step backward is backing up. Pick up the reins; shift your weight back a little, and once he takes a step back you can release the pressure. Continue working with that until he backs up for as long as you want.

By teaching your horse consistent commands that always has the same meaning, the horse will eventually know what to do. No matter what it is, like getting in a trailer, or lunging.

CHAPTER 9: HOW TO CONTROL YOUR HORSE

There are some people who try to lead their horse by controlling their head with a lead rope. This result will be your horse pulling or jerking the lead rope and pulling back or pushing around the person holding the lead rope.

There should be some slack in the lead rope as you are leading your horse because you don't want to pull or jerk him. When your horse moves the wrong way, you will then stop and make him move the right way by making him move his body.

To secret to successfully controlling your horse is to have control over your horse's body. To do this, control his feet by making him move his rear end away from you. This is also known as disengaging the hindquarters. This works well because it will alleviate stiffness and tension while almost force your horse to focus on you.

There are several methods you can use to get your horse to move his rear end away from you. Most of the time you can stand facing his shoulder and point to his hip. If he doesn't move keep pointing and cluck at him. Tap him with the lead rope while clucking at him if he still doesn't move.

When he does move, take the pressure off him immediately. Make sure to pat him and tell him "Good Boy!" Then ask for another move. Then you will repeat it all again and ask for more steps. You will need to remember to do this on both sides of the body. It won't be long before you will simply point at his hip and he will move them for you.

After you have moved him, turn your body to walk forward while holding your lead line. If he messes up all you have to do is move his rear end again. If your horse starts getting ahead of you while you are leading him move his hindquarters. You will repeat the same action if your horse starts lagging behind you. Every time he deviates from your side, you will repeat the process of moving his hindquarters. It won't be long and your horse will start gauging your pace and keep up with you at the same pace.

Good control when leading your horse is the most basic training techniques there is. It is also the method by which you can get your horse into a trailer, moving them around, bathing them, and even riding them. Your horse will learn through these techniques to be soft and responsive. If your horse is soft and responsive while you are on the ground, you will have the same kind of horse when you are in the saddle.

CHAPTER 10: HOW TO LOAD A HORSE INTO A TRAILER

Loading your horse onto a trailer is one of life's many challenges. That is especially true if your horse isn't sure that is where he wants to go. Loading a horse onto a trailer can be dangerous if people become frustrated and impatient, and then they start trying to yank or shove an unwilling horse into the trailer. A frightened or annoyed horse can start lashing out with his hooves or just mashing you into the side of the trailer.

There are ways to teach a horse to load into a trailer and your horse's smooth progress into the trailer will depend largely on your patience and the horse's history.

If your horse has had a horrifying experience being loaded into a trailer, such as someone pushed, abused or roped it to get it in the trailer, it will take more work to get your horse accustom to going up the ramp and into a dark trailer. Of course if you start this training early in their life, you will have a horse that thinks it is

28

perfectly normal to get onto the trailer to go somewhere.

It is now up to you to convince your horse that walking up a ramp into an enclosed space is normal and safe. Do not get in the trailer and attempt to lead him in. Trying that method has injured many people. The general idea is to get him to walk into the trailer on his own steam. Take the lead in your left hand and give the command, "Walk". You may have to walk him up part way and then stop, then finish the rest of the way in. He may try to back up. If he does, let him and then start all over again.

You will need a lot of patience to repeat this process. You will need to have more patience than your horse to win and have your horse loaded. If you let your horse win, he will always challenge going into the trailer. So when he backs out, remember your patience. You won't take a break, leaving him to think he has won. You will patiently, walk him back into that trailer until he realizes that you are not going to give up on this event. He will understand that he's going to keep walking up that ramp until the end of time or until he is safely loaded in the trailer.

If you must, tap your horse on the rump to get him to move forward. Don't ever hit your horse inside the trailer; it is dangerous for both of you. Also never hit him as long as he is doing what you ask. Once he has obeyed, make sure to praise him and let him rest. This will let him know that what he did was right and the monotony will stop.

Be sure you practice loading at different times of the day. Loading at night isn't any different than loading in the daytime.

CHAPTER 11: ANOTHER METHOD FOR TRAINING A HORSE TO LOAD INTO A TRAILER

Since there is no one right way or one wrong way to train a horse, you may want to change the method you are using to train your horse. If you are not having any luck with one method you can always try another.

Here is another method of training your horse to go into a trailer.

Regardless of the training method you are using you must have good communication between you and your horse. It is necessary for the horse to understand what you want him to do and you must make it easy for the horse to understand what you want him to do.

Once the horse gets good at moving both directions then it is time to hook a lead rope to his halter and lunge him left and right. Just as an example, when you point left you want the horse to go to your left, and when you point right you want the horse to go to your right.

The end result will be this. You are holding the lead rope while facing your horse. While you are holding the lead rope in your right hand, you will hook the lead rope in your left thumb. Lift the rope to the where the horse can see it and point to the left.

Because your horse knows what to do, he will immediately go to your left. After a circle or two you will switch hands and using the same motions will make your horse go to your right.

After your horse has mastered that, send him or lunge him through a gate opening, barn door opening, etc. You will also want to use smaller spaces to lunge him through to give him the opportunity to deal with his natural claustrophobia. You can accomplish this by lunging him between you and a fence. As he goes back and forth from left to right make the space between you and the fence smaller. Take care you don't get stepped on.

Once he has mastered that, you can take him by the trailer. Open the door to the trailer and allow him a chance to sniff it. Then you will step back and while facing your horse, you will lunge him to the left and to the right in front of the trailer as he passes back and forth by the opening.

After all the pointing and sending your horse knows what you want. You have communicated to him when you point to the left he is to move to the left and so on.

The next step will be to make him face the trailer. With his head facing into the trailer and you standing on his left side you will then point and send him into the trailer. Some horses will simply jump right in the trailer where others may take more work.

If your horse will not go into the trailer after pointing and persuading, take him away from the trailer and make him work. Now you are transmitting the idea that being in the trailer means he gets to relax. Being outside the trailer means he has to work hard. Sooner or later he will catch on.

After you get him into the trailer, you need to pet him and let him relax. You want to let him know how well he did, so praise him.

CHAPTER 12: 5 COMMON MISTAKES TO AVOID WHEN LOADING A HORSE

Mistake #1 – Thinking your horse is like a dog or a cat

Unless the new horse owner has been educated, they may think their horse is like a cat or dog. The new horse owner may pat his thigh and say, "C'mon" a few times and the horse will just leap into the trailer like a happy dog.

Mistake #2 – Using food as bait

Another mistake new horse owners often make is putting hay, grain, apples or some other food at the front of the trailer to tempt a horse to step in to get the food. This almost never works. If it did, it would be a stroke of luck. Some horses will lean in and try to get the food, but they won't step into the trailer if their life depended on it.

Mistake #3 – Forgetting to hook the trailer to the truck

Some new horse owners will forget the hitch the trailer to the truck before trying to get the horse into the trailer. With the trailer unhooked, when the horse steps into the trailer, the trailer is going to wobble around. This is going to spook the horse making it more difficult to get him into a trailer the next time.

Mistake #4 – Starting a "Tug-o-War" with your horse

Some people will try to pull on the lead rope to get their horse into the trailer. This turns into a classic game of "tug-o-war". Now who do you think is going to win, you or the thousand pound creature you are pulling on?

Getting a horse loaded into a trailer is a challenge, but trying this method will only frustrate you or get you hurt.

Mistake #5 – Going trail riding before the horse is good at loading into a trailer

Many horse owners will get their horse into the trailer once and think that training is over. So when they decide to go trail riding, the horse won't get back into the trailer. The main reason for this is because they did not practice getting on and off the trailer enough to make it a routine.

CHAPTER 13: PROPER TRAINING TECHNIQUES CAN CURE BEHAVIOR ISSUES

If you have not studied horse training, it can be a mystifying subject. Even more of a puzzle is a horse with a behavioral problem. Behavioral issues cause stress and frustration for owners. Many people don't understand that the behavioral problem is usually the fault of the trainer not the horse.

The first step is unscrambling the horse's behavior. As an example, many riders experienced a horse being spooked. This means the horse is nervous and afraid something is going to "get him." Every time the horse and rider go for a ride it is not relaxing for either one of them.

Let's assume the rider is causing the horse to spook, so we must find out how the rider is doing this. An inexperienced rider may not be aware that he is sitting tensely in the saddle. He also may be stiff as a board and has white-knuckles from gripping the reins so tightly. The horse can sense these things and will feel the same tension the rider is feeling. The horse may become spooked by this and the rider senses the horse's reaction and becomes more alarmed. The rider and the horse are intensifying each other's fears to the point where their anxieties will grow by leaps and bounds.

The rider is human and has the capability of reasoning. So it is up to the rider to stop irrational behavior first in him and then in the horse. You must loosen up in the saddle. If you relax and have fun, the horse will relax and signal that he notices a change. Then you need to talk to him and build his confidence. The horse's behavior will soon change and the end result will be a more relaxed and fun to ride horse.

Whether or not the rider is aware of it, he or she is training the horse by just riding him. Remember every time you interact with your horse you are training him. The horse will react to the encouragement he gets. If the encouragement is consistent, the horse's reaction will become a habit. If the stimulus is tense, it causes fear and results in a spooky horse.

This is just one example of how you can be the reason for the horse's behavior. Now this is not true 100% of the time, but it is a good place to start unraveling the problem. In most cases it is where the problem began.

Chapter 14: How to Teach Your Horse to Perform Longer Sliding Stops

Once your horse is consistently stopping in one stride and sliding a couple of feet when you say, "whoa", you can begin to teach him to do a longer sliding stop. Before you start this training make sure your horse is good at the short sliding stops, so that you will have a foundation to build on.

The length of your horse's slide is established by several factors. They are as follows:

- The horse's natural ability and aptitude for stopping
- The type of ground you are riding on
- The horse's shoes
- The rate of speed the horse is going into the stop

- The manner the rider cues the horse to stop, rein work and posture

Each one of the above factors affects your horse's slide.

It is important to understand almost any horse has the ability to perform a little two-footed slide on good ground. Not every horse is able to learn to slide fifteen or twenty feet. For you to accomplish this, the horse must have both the ability and the desire to learn to stop and slide.

Trying to train a horse to make a long sliding stop that isn't so inclined to making that kind of stop will have the end results of your training sessions becoming harsh and unpleasant for both of you. Your horse could end up being frightened of you and it still won't stop well on a consistent basis. So it's important to make sure that your horse wants to become a long-slide stopper.

So how will you be able to tell if he wants to learn? If stopping while at a trot or a slow lope was easy for him to learn, there is a good chance you will be able to train him to become a long-slide stopper. This is assuming you have advanced the stop gradually and your horse has the physical strength to hold a hard stop.

On the other hand, if you have had a difficult time training your horse to stop at a trot or slow lope, it's not worth trying to teach him to advance the stop. He will resist the training and both of you will end up frustrated.

The ground is another factor that affects how well the horse can slide. Long slides just won't happen on the wrong kind of ground. Good sliding ground is ground that consists of a hard, smooth packed base with two to three inches of loose dirt on top. This gives your horse the advantage of a solid base to slide on, which will stop him from digging in his hooves too deep and shortening his slide. It must be smooth or your horse's feet might catch in a rut. This could shorten the slide or injure your horse.

The loose, fluffy dirt on top of the base will soften the impact of the feet hitting the hard base. Without this cushion your horse can become sore. The loose dirt is easy for your horse to plough through while sliding. If the top layer is too deep or heavy, your horse won't be able to slide far. He will also need outstanding strength to hold a slide in deep, heavy dirt.

You can improve your sliding ground by adding rice hulls or shavings to it. This will make the top layer a lot more light and fluffy.

The shoes your horse is shod with will also have an impact on his ability to slide. You must use sliding shoes made of tempered, flat bar iron. They are about one inch to an inch and a half wide. The wider they are, the less friction they have on the ground and the longer the slide.

The nails of the horseshoe are counter sunk, so that they are flush with the shoe. This helps to reduce friction. The front quarter inch of the shoe is curved upward a lot like the beginning end of a snow ski. This will prevent the horse's toes from jamming or catching on the ground while they are sliding. The shoe's quarters should come almost straight back from the curve of the toe, which will allow dirt to flow easily out the back.

The trailers of the shoe should not extend back to, but not past, the bulbs of the foot. You need to trim the hind feet with a slightly longer toes and lower heel than usual. You are doing this to create more surface area on the hooves and increase the potential of the slide. It also reduces the danger of the horse catching his toe in the dirt, which will send him knuckling in the dirt and injuring himself. These slight changes are good, but don't make the mistake of thinking MORE is better. Trimming the heels too high will cause the horse to knuckle over and pull a tendon while trying to stop. Trimming the heels too low you will run the risk that he will strain a hamstring.

The build of your horse is also important. The horses with the greater advantage for sliding have straight hind legs and feet that point straight ahead. Their feet are able to stay together during a slide. However when the horse's back feet toe out will begin to spread as the horse goes into a slide and the longer the slide the farther out the hind legs will spread. He will have to come out of the slide to bring his feet back together.

If a horse has this problem, he will make V shaped slide tracks. The horse's owner can correct this just by slightly turning the horseshoe so it points straight ahead. It can also help to rock the toe just a little toward the inside of the foot.

The speed your horse is running when it goes into the stop is a most important factor in determining the length of the slide. For example, if you want your horse to do a sliding stop the length of the arena floor, you will start at a slow speed and gradually build up speed, a little with each stride, until you ask for the stop.

You must ask for the stop during the horse's acceleration. During the acceleration, your horse's shoulders will be more elevated and his back feet will reach further beneath him. Both of these things are necessary fundamentals for a good long slide.

Make sure you carefully time his acceleration. You don't want the horse to be moving too fast when you ask for the stop. If he is going too fast he may ignore the signal to stop. A horse's instinct will let the horse know how fast they can run and still attempt a stop. By making him run faster, he will concentrate more on the running and forget about the upcoming stop. He might not have the strength to hold a hard stop over a certain speed and in essence he won't try it. Plenty of practice and experimenting will help you to find your horse's optimum running speed for a long stop.

Remember; don't ask your horse to hard stop from his top-speed too often. He will sour if you do. Always remember to use skid boots to protect his fetlocks during the skid.

Having your horse accelerate too quickly, then begin to slow as you near the stop; you will usually have a disappointing slide. The horse is decelerating when you ask for the stop, so there is no need to do it twice.

You must ask your horse for a stop while the horse is running on a straightaway, never during a turn or curving. The horse's body should also be aligned straight as if an imaginary line were drawn from the tip of his nose to the end of his tail when you ask for a stop. If your horse is even slightly crooked when you ask him to stop, he will not be in balance during the stop, which can be dangerous for both of you. To ensure a straight stop, make sure he's running a straight path down the arena, not veering or zigzagging.

The method used by the rider to cue the stop is critical. The reins must be used correctly, have perfect timing, and great posture to enable your horse to slide a long distance. It is just as important to know what not to do as it is to the correct method to use.

Pulling harder on the reins will produce a shorter slide, instead of a longer one. The reason is because the hard pull makes your horse spread his hind legs too far and jam his feet too deeply into the ground to slide that far. A horse needs the use of his head and neck for balance in a long slide, and he won't have that if the rider is yanking on the reins.

There are three techniques you can try to do this correctly. You may need to try all three, but then the first one may work. Each horse responses differently which is the reason for the three different techniques. It will be your task to find the technique that works the best for you and your horse.

When stopping your horse for a slide, the best way is to keep slack in the reins and say, "Whoa!" This signals your horse slide as long as possible, because the rider is not interfering with him. Just remember to use light pressure, do not pull. Without the distraction of the reins being pulled, he can slide as far as he wants. For this method to be effective, your horse has to want to stop and enjoys the slide. The average horse will more than likely stop than not stop this way consistently.

Another method is to say; "Whoa!" while applying light pressure on the reins, then let your horse slide with no more interference from you. You must use light pressure and do not pull. By applying a pound or two of pressure and setting your hand solid, without pulling or allowing slack in the reins, will allow your horse to slide as far as he can.

This last technique will usually work on the majority of horses. When you ask for the stop, say, "Whoa!", wait just a split second, then apply rein pressure, set your hand, and allow slack in the reins, but only an inch or two, not too much. Almost immediately the horse will go into the stop. The horse will continue to slide with the reins slack.

Set your hand again, if you feel your horse start to release the stop and then again slack the reins once more. This set, slack maneuver repeats throughout the entire slide until the horse has come to a complete stop.

The whole whoa-set-slack technique seems to work well because after giving the verbal cue, waiting just a split second gives the horse a chance to enter the slide on his own. His hooves enter the ground more smoothly than they would if he was startled by the "whoa" and rein pressure at the same time.

When the horse's hooves are set and sliding, the short pressure with the reins will remind him to stay in the slide. Immediately slacking the reins, allows the horse to slide as far as he wants. If you were to keep constant pressure, this would cause the horse's hooves to dig into deep and prematurely end the slide. It can also cause the horse to become rigid and pull.

If the horse tries to stop the slide the quick set-slack reminds him to remain in the slide. Do not set the reins again unless you feel the horse has begun to come out of the slide. Considering a long slide only takes a few seconds, this set-slack also happens very rapidly. The rider must pay attention to the feel of the horse to get this one right.

One last key element the rider must do to cue the stop is to relax his body. You will use your body to generate energy and help the hose accelerate forward as you ride. When you ask for the stop, you must also stop. To be more specific, you must sit down, stop the movements of riding and relax in the saddle with your back, shoulders and thighs limp.

As your body relaxes, it is a stopping cue your horse will instantly recognize and respond to. Timing is an important key. Keep riding until you cue that stop, or your horse will recognize the change in body language and will stop too early. This can ruin the slide.

The posture of your body is very important in getting the best possible slide from your horse. It will take practice. You and your horse will not be doing any lengthy slide overnight. Just remember to concentrate and keep practicing. You both will have it together sooner or later.

MEET THE AUTHOR

Lifetime Horse enthusiast Sue Jordan helps clients train and care for their horses. Owning a horse is no small commitment (literally or figuratively). A horse with good training will be a friend for life; however a poorly-trained horse will be a lifelong headache. Sue loves helping owners and families enjoy their time with these majestic creatures.

Sue grew up around horses. Her father owned a horse farm and studded horses, so she was often able to watch a horse grow up from the moment of birth. The process created a deep sense of respect and awe in her, and she channeled that into becoming a trainer who exercises a kind but firm hand in the training process.

After almost two decades in the training business, Sue has discovered that there is a *huge* benefit when owners are involved in the training process itself.

Sue lives in Atlanta, Georgia on her family's farm. Her husband Ron took over the business years ago, but she and her father still enjoy peaceful rides on the property. When she's not working with horses or writing, she is also an avid quilter.

CPSIA information can be obtained
at www.ICGtesting.com
Printed in the USA
LVHW06s1318140518
577109LV00014B/378/P

9 781634 281270